UNDERSTANDING
SANTA FE
REAL ESTATE

♠ ♠ ♠ ♠ ♠ ♠ ♠ ♠ ♠ ♠ ♠ ♠ ♠

KAREN WALKER

Drawings by Jerome Milord

Ancient City Press
Santa Fe, New Mexico

International Standard Book Number:
0-91270-61-0 paperback

Library of Congress Catalogue Number:
89-081748

Cover art by Glen T. Strock
Drawings by Jerome Milord
Book design by Mary Powell
Cover design by Don Cuary

CONTENTS

My thanks to:

— Residents and hopeful buyers who told me what they still didn't understand about the oddities of Santa Fe custom and practice.

— Hope Aldrich and Bob Mayer of the *Reporter* who not only published these articles but endured my allergy to editing.

— My sons, Pat and Jim, and my two Karens, who pointed out when some idea was not clear.

— Brian Dennehy, who first suggested that these articles become a book.

— Doug Schwartz, who encouraged the concept and my efforts, and said "just start with the paper in the typewriter."

— Susan and David Jones, friends and members of a Santa Fe ditch association, for their comments on "Acequias."

— My attorney, John Jasper, who has no liability here but over many years has honed my sense of legal detail.

— Ancient City Press who believed, as I do, that this book has a function for property buyers in Santa Fe.

PREFACE

This collection of articles is intended for the potential buyer of real property in the Santa Fe area. The comprehensive range of subjects discussed in brief should suggest an array of informed questions before a purchase agreement is signed. Answers to further peculiarities of property in Santa Fe should be provided by a broker and/or real estate attorney, each knowledgeable in local, current custom and law, and above all possessed of integrity.

As a resident of Santa Fe since 1970 and owner-broker of Karen Walker Real Estate, with offices at La Posada since 1973, I have long been aware of the unique and sometimes historically-based challenges facing Santa Fe property buyers. More recently, I have served as vice-chair of the Urban Policy Committee of the City of Santa Fe Planning Commission and as chair of this city's Urban Design Committee. Both positions have brought me to a heightened awareness of environment-enhancing ordinances, such as our Open Space Plan and Escarpment and Terrain Management regulations.

This combination of experience, property broker and city appointee, has honed my sense of the need to express to buyers the issues we hold dear in this community, as well as some unique facets of law or custom.

So the response was ready and natural when in September, 1988, Hope Aldrich, publisher of the weekly *Santa Fe Reporter*, asked if I would write a column on property for their livelihood section. The first articles appeared in October. Soon readers began suggesting additional topics, and by December Brian Dennehy urged me to compile the pieces into a book. The first compilation was distributed privately. During the late summer of 1989, it was expanded and edited for this Ancient City Press publication, which has been illustrated by Jerome Milord.

Northern New Mexico is a fascinating area, one where the land has been settled and farmed and enjoyed for centuries. This antiquity has its own legacy. Here it is not uncommon for land to be handed down through generations of a family, with little attention to courthouse recording systems or accurate boundary surveys. There may even be multiple claims to ownership of the same tract of land. For these reasons, a clean title insurance policy is a necessity for future peace of mind.

If you are one of the many people thinking of buying land in northern New Mexico for an investment or for a future home, here are some questions you should consider asking the seller, your broker and your attorney:

One of the first questions should be that of access to the property. The fact that a road exists and you have driven on it to the available parcel does not automatically mean you have legal access to that parcel. Anyone with a blader can create a road! Check for a recorded and permanent easement (the right to limited use of someone else's property) to the land you hope to buy. Or if none exists, check if the road is owned and maintained by the city or county.

If the road is a private easement, and not public, make sure that there is a shared road and maintenance agreement for all users of the road. This will detail your rights and obligations. If no agreement exists, request that the seller provide one.

If you hope to obtain a loan to purchase the land at a later time, institutional lenders currently require this sort of agreement. Be sure you understand and are comfortable with the assurances and obligations of this document.

Another question you should consider is whether the parcel is a legal lot of record. Has it been split off from a larger parcel? It may have been split in good faith, but without the owner having gone through the requirements imposed by the city or county on the subdivision process.

If the property has been subdivided, request a copy of the subdivision plat. If you expect that certain utilities will be provided, make sure that the appropriate signatures of these utility companies appear on the plat as well as those of the city or county. The plat should be on record in the county courthouse or city hall. Look for recording data (book and page) and a seal.

If the lot is outside the city, was the land subdivided after the County Development Code of January 1981? If it's inside the city, does the lot meet the minimum size for the area's zoning? If not, is it "grandfathered," or created before zoning regulations came into being? If the land is not a "legal lot," you will have trouble getting a building permit.

Does the seller really own what he is purporting to sell? It can happen that the seller has unintentionally shown you and his broker the wrong parcel of land. He may have been out of this area for a long time and honestly forgotten the exact location of the property he bought 15 years ago. The way to ensure that you are in fact buying what you are being shown is to request a new boundary survey with the corners staked and flagged. This is a necessity *before* you pay for the land, not afterward.

Imagine that you are in the process of purchasing real property. For some time you have been working with a broker or salesperson, and you have developed rapport and confidence in one another. Together you have seen several properties. This broker has provided you with a wealth of valuable information such as comparable prices, financing strategy, surveys, title insurance details and other items of significance for your decision. You become good friends. This broker could even be a family member.

Then further imagine your surprise upon learning that this broker with whom you have worked so closely is the legal "agent" of the seller. This is so even if he or she has never been introduced to the seller and has no personal knowledge of the seller. How does this happen?

Agency refers to a set of laws governing the relationship between a principal and his agent. In New Mexico, the law as enforced by the New Mexico Real Estate Commission defines an agent's principal as "The person from whom the agent's commission or fee is received." This concept is difficult for brokers, attorneys and others to remember when a broker is clearly closer to the buyer and his concerns. Customarily, however,

the seller pays the commissions and is therefore the principal.

As a buyer, the broker with whom you have been working owes you honesty and fairness and must represent the property's condition truthfully. But as an agent of the seller, he or she owes even more to the principal, including such duties as confidentiality. The broker who has been showing property to you may learn that a seller is willing to accept less than the listed or offered price. Without the permission of the principal (seller) this broker may not pass on this information, however helpful to you.

New Mexico is one of the few states that interprets an agency relationship in this strictly defined manner.

In California, as the buyer, you may request that "your" broker represent you, even though he receives compensation from the seller. Of course, this relationship needs to be defined in writing.

But you are in New Mexico. What are your options?

You can rely on the honesty and good will of the broker or sales person who is showing property to you and be comfortable with the relationship. Or you can consider a buyer-agency contract. This contract is one in which you compensate the broker either on a fixed fee basis or as a percentage of the purchase price. In this case, the broker works solely for you and your interests and has no fiduciary, or trusteeship obligation to the seller. A reliable attorney specializing in real estate is the best source of counsel on this matter.

In the Santa Fe area, any real property which you own or are thinking of purchasing or leasing will have some restraints placed upon your use of it. Crucial to your decisions as a buyer is knowledge of these restraints, also known as zoning and covenants. As a seller, you need to know how to represent your property.

All real property in our city and county is governed by some form of zoning. Some properties are further controlled by private covenants and/or deed restrictions, which will be reviewed in the following chapter.

Zoning restraints include such things as setbacks of construction from lot lines; height or elevation restrictions; the percentage of your building site you can cover with improvements; minimum lot size; and purpose of usage, e.g. residential or commercial.

Some questions our zoning regulations answer are: Can you work at home? Can a church or school be constructed in your neighborhood? Can you sell from your home the dogs which you breed? If some utilities are not available in your area, can you drill a well or install a septic tank? Where can you operate a "bed and breakfast"?

In Santa Fe County, probably the major form of restraint is ground water availability. Ground water is

that which we need to drill for, as distinct from surface water. Availability and supply of ground water determines density, which is a form of zoning.

"Density" tells us the minimum lot size allowable for construction. Because of varying amounts of ground water, one area of the county may require a minimum of five acres for a home site. Another area may require a minimum of 12.5 acres. The County Development Code is a necessary initial guide for your research.

Historically, zoning came about as a health and safety protection for city residents. Many of the populace in Eastern cities were living in tenements, deprived of adequate light and air. Zoning helped assure that future construction allowed for healthier conditions, including the absence of polluting industry in residential areas.

"Zoning" is an expression which means that an authority of government, with the concurrence of citizens, has determined your use as owner, or lessee, of real property. In the city of Santa Fe a zoning code was adopted in the early 1950s, but was not enforced because the city had no staff. The Zoning Ordinance of 1962, with ongoing changes and embellishments, is our current code.

Changes have occurred from population pressures, neighborhood requests and generally changing needs. Additions have proceeded partly from recognition of historical uses. For example, the AC, or Arts and Crafts zoning, recognizes the history of persons selling art-related objects from their homes. Canyon Road and part of Old Santa Fe Trail are zoned AC.

Another after-the-fact recognition is Compound zoning. This acknowledges common walls and zero set-backs from the lot line, peculiar to our oldest sections of Santa Fe.

The City of Santa Fe enforces its zoning regulations. A few years ago a homeowner was required to remove his third story because its height violated the ordinance. If you attempt a non-conforming use, size or design, your building permit will not be forthcoming.

There is a difference of opinion on the philosophy of zoning. Some feel its main function is to preserve the status quo. Others believe zoning safeguards our environment and quality of life. If you have questions, you will find City Hall informative and helpful. Call Dean Hunt, director of Code Enforcement, or Ed Romero, director of Zoning Division within Code Enforcement.

What are private covenants or deed restrictions? They are controls and limitations on the use of real property, and are imposed on that property by an individual rather than a government entity.

In the previous chapter, I discussed some common forms of governmental control, which are zoning and the determination of utility use. These devices are used to regulate and manage growth.

Private covenants are rarely imposed with the intention of regulating growth. They tend to proceed from aesthetic interests, or the desire to retain the character of a beloved neighborhood in which one has lived. Sometimes the owner has an interest in adjacent property and hopes to enhance its future value.

These covenants or restrictions are imposed by the owner of a property who at some time in the future intends to sell or convey to another. This owner hopes to control the future use of the land in a more restrictive way than it is controlled by the current governmental authority.

An owner's aesthetic concerns are sometimes expressed by restrictions on the height of construction, so that a future building not loom large on an otherwise

attractive skyline. Or perhaps an interesting topography could be best preserved by specifying the building location on the land.

If an owner has an interest in adjacent property, he is likely to impose restrictions that he feels will ensure the future value of the adjacent land. Again, these could include height restrictions so as not to block the view. Or where city zoning calls for a 35-foot building setback from a lot line, the owner may impose a 50-foot setback. This would ensure greater privacy for future home sites, and presumably a higher future value for the land.

An interesting form of restriction is one in which the grantor or donor of land requires a specific use, such as land given for the Amelia White Park or for the governor's mansion. If these lands do not continue to be used in the way specified by the covenant, the property reverts or returns to the original donor or heirs.

Private covenants or deed restrictions run for a specific period of time, then lapse if not renewed. As mentioned, they tend to be more restrictive than a municipality's zoning requirements. But while the city enforces its own zoning codes, it does not enforce private restrictions. This is left to the grantor (seller), or sometimes to neighbors. A few years ago the City of Santa Fe gave permission for a certain lot split. The neighbors researched the covenants, found they did not allow such a split, and brought suit to require that the buyer leave the land in one piece.

Most buyers like the restrictive covenants for the same reason the seller imposed them. However, be sure you are comfortable with them before you purchase. Restrictions are outlined in the deed conveying title; or if detailed in another document, they are referred to in the deed. Check your preliminary title report, which is issued before you purchase. If any private covenants exist, this report will note them, and the title company will provide you with a copy of them.

With the purchase of real property comes an exhilarating sense of freedom of ownership—your own home or land. However, are you inadvertently becoming part of a homeowners' association?

A homeowners' association is likely to be formed whenever some element is held in common by more than one owner. These elements can be simply greenbelt areas or common roads; or perhaps, at the maximum, an entire condominium project's common elements.

The developers of the land or land and structures will incorporate a homeowners' association. This association will be governed by bylaws and a declaration of covenants, conditions and restrictions (CC & R's).

The bylaws define membership in the homeowners' association, selection of the board of directors, and powers and duties of this board. The article in the bylaws most worthy of your attention is titled "Assessments," including both annual and special assessments for capital improvements. What percentage of owners is needed to levy these assessments or to change their amounts, usually upward? Can the directors put the association into debt for some expense you

feel is frivolous? And at what stage in the sale of the development do the developers give control of the association to the homeowners?

Sometimes the developers retain control, including control over assessments, until 75 percent of the properties are sold. Determine what percentage of members is needed to amend these bylaws.

The declaration of CC & R's is intended to "protect the value and standards of said real estate." This protection includes aesthetic and often environmental considerations. The assessment powers are further delineated in this document. But also outlined are restrictions on your use, which may cause dismay later if you don't read these CC & R's before your purchase.

In some developments, guest houses are disallowed. Or perhaps you always wanted to build a two-story home, only to find that there is a height limit of 15 feet.

Is there a restriction on the number of deciduous trees per building site? Are you in a development area where the cubic footage of water in a swimming pool will be regulated? Or possibly no pools of any size are allowed? Many covenants allow no more than two dogs and/or cats per household.

Common to all homeowners' associations are monthly fees. These can amount to a modest $20 a month to maintain a greenbelt area. Or the fees may be a few hundred dollars a month to service recreational facilities and security devices, common utilities and insurance.

Before your purchase of real property in a "development," obtain all the documents created by the developer and request that your attorney give you an opinion. Also determine if the development is approved by "Fannie Mae" or the Federal National Mortgage Association. If not, you may find that borrowing opportunities are limited. Also be aware that an authority of government may disagree with a CC & R's allowance of a guest house, due to dwindling ground water supplies.

An advantage of homeowners' associations is that some functions are cared for by others, such as road or recreational facility maintenance. Some disadvantages are a loss of sovereignty or the obligation to pay for facilities you don't want. Your primary concern should be, on balance, your comfort with the association's concepts.

When purchasing real property, how can you be assured that you are receiving clear and unfettered title to this property?

In the Santa Fe area, an Abstract of Title was the most common form of assurance until the early 1970s. An Abstract of Title is a written history of the chain of ownership of land, and incidentally can provide fascinating reading.

The practice was to present this history to your attorney for review, specifically to search for gaps or errors in the chain of ownership. If your attorney approved your Abstract, you completed your purchase in the confidence that your title would not be challenged.

Since that time, however, the common method of warranting a clear title to property has become that of Title Insurance. Your policy is issued by a Title Guaranty Company through your local Abstract and Title company, which searches the Santa Fe County courthouse records. This search is intended to discover any liens, defects or encroachments against the property you hope to purchase. If problems are found in this search of the courthouse records, the seller will attempt to clear them up. If the problems can't be solved or the situation changed, these defects will appear in your insurance policy as "exceptions to coverage."

Keep in mind that a title guaranty company, like any insurance company, prefers to pay as few claims as possible. So the page of exceptions to insurance coverage, known as Schedule B-II, should receive your full attention. Schedule B-II will include 10 standard exceptions to your title insurance coverage plus other exceptions pertaining particularly to your new property.

In the Santa Fe area, it is customary for the seller to provide and pay for the title policy. When drafting your offer to purchase, include the contingency that the seller deliver a policy with two of the standard exceptions deleted from the Schedule B-II. These exceptions are the ones relating to the survey and to liens. If these exceptions are not deleted, you may find the title insurance company unwilling to pay a claim related to an inaccurate survey or a roofer's lien unpaid by your seller. Deleting these exceptions will be an added cost to the seller, but offers protection for both of you.

Also recommended is deletion of exceptions 1 and 2. These relate to rights of parties in possession and to easements.

Schedule B-II's non-standard exceptions, or those particular to your property, can prove quite interesting. You may find that a corner of the living room encroaches or overlaps on the neighbor's land. Or that others have been crossing your intended property for years, without the owner's permission or any formal easement agreement. If your land doesn't front on a public road, does the policy list access as an exception to coverage?

Upon tendering your offer to purchase, request a preliminary title insurance policy right away. Some problems leading to exceptions to coverage can be solved and the exceptions deleted from your insurance policy. Make sure you can live with those conditions that can't be changed. If you or your attorney disapprove of these latter, don't buy the property.

CITY UTILITIES 7

There are so many attractive areas in our county. Before you set your heart and your property search in one location or another, consider the cost, quality and availability of utilities.

Within the city limits the City of Santa Fe provides only a sewer system. Santa Fe is one of the few New Mexico cities which does not own its own water system. Public Service Company of New Mexico (PNM) provides water and electricity. PNM also owns the Gas Company and so is our natural gas supplier. However, not all of these utilities are to be found in some areas even though such areas are within the city.

Much of the property north of the Governor's Mansion features no sewer. Instead, septic systems are the state of the art. Most of the land (and homes) from St. John's College east to the National Forest have neither sewer, PNM water, nor natural gas available to them. Some areas of the city exceed the maximum elevation above which PNM is not required to deliver water, and so wells are used.

There are various reasons for the lack of utilities in parts of our city. Among them are topographical problems such as elevation or not enough gravity flow, which

20

would hinder a sewer system. Another reason is the lack of easements. That is, there may be no legal right for a utility supplier to cross over or under private property to service that or adjacent parcels.

What if the utility systems you would expect to be found within the city are not available to you? Make sure you are comfortable with the alternatives, their cost and quality before you proceed with a purchase. Can you accept well water instead of PNM water; a septic system instead of sewer; propane gas and electricity rather than natural gas for heating and cooking? A talk with people already using these alternative systems may reassure you.

The next chapter will look at utility considerations in Santa Fe County, outside our city limits.

Do your preferences in real property lean toward larger land spaces...three, five, ten acres or more? If so, you are likely concentrating your property search outside our city limits, and looking in the Santa Fe County area.

In the county, PNM water and natural gas are available only in unusual situations such as a trade of easements (the legal right to cross another's property) for utility hook-ups. In most cases, in the county, a buyer and/or builder will be living with a well for water delivery. Heating and cooking needs will be supplied through propane gas, electricity, solar or some combination of these energy sources. Sewage disposal will require the installation of a septic system.

None of these alternative utility systems should be considered a negative factor. But you will be assuming an individual responsibility for the maintenance of these, your own systems. So before purchasing you should engage in some preliminary investigations which can alert you as to costs and quality of your utilities.

What is the cost of drilling and casing a well? Add a pressure tank, a pump, and a delivery line from the well to your home site. Include these costs in your property budget. If a well is already in place, hire a hydrol-

ogist to test the well for GPM or "gallons per minute" of water delivery. Is it sufficient for the number of appliances you intend to operate or for your always-showering teenagers? Also test for potability and noxious chemicals.

Is your well water supply subject to any existing lawsuit? Is the well shared with another land owner? If so, you must be comfortable with a shared well agreement. In any case, ask your attorney to review relevant data.

Other utility questions to ask or determine for yourself are:

Is the soil suitable for a septic system (such that percolation is possible for a septic leach field); what is the cost of propane gas; how long need you wait for phone service; is electric service available at or near the building site? When construction begins you will need an electric transformer. This device transfers energy from one circuit to another with a change in voltage, or current, and can cost a considerable sum.

If you decide that your utility costs and quality are within an acceptable limit, enjoy the space and views.

MLS is the abbreviation for Multiple Listing Service. This system is sponsored by your local Board of Realtors, and subscribed to and paid for by its membership. It gathers and disseminates information about nearly every property available for purchase in your area. This is because, in Santa Fe, most brokers and salespersons are Realtors. That is, they have joined the Board of Realtors and therefore support this information system.

Data is supplied by the property's owner and submitted to the system through the member real estate brokerage firm. Property categories include, among other things, residential, vacant land, commercial and income properties, parcels in and out of the city, and farms and ranches.

All data is published twice monthly in the "MLS" book purchased by Realtors. In addition, daily updates are available via your Realtor's terminal, which is connected to the mainframe at the Board of Realtor's office.

The most important decision which you will make, as a buyer or seller, is your selection of a broker. Choose someone who is honest, intelligent and reliable. Another critical element to your success is your use of the Multiple Listing Service, which implies that your broker is also a member of the Board of Realtors.

As a seller, this system exposes your property to the widest market, the greatest number of buyers. As a buyer, you have access to the largest selection of properties available for purchase.

In some areas of the country there is no active MLS. A buyer needs to contact the listing firm or whoever's name is on a sign, even if you have found a broker with whom you prefer to work. In Santa Fe, you can see any property in Multiple Listing through a single Realtor of your choice and enjoy the comfort of an established and preferred relationship.

This property information is only as good as the reliability and thoroughness of input from the owner and the owner's broker. However, the Multiple Listing Service is an essential clearinghouse of data and is a benefit to you whether you are buying or selling.

Do you own property, or anticipate owning property within the city limits of Santa Fe? If so, the time will come when you have questions concerning the options for that property's use. Some likely questions are "Can I sell off part of my lot?"; "Can I add a second story?"; or, "Is it possible to work out of my home?" Other common inquires include the requirements of building codes, setbacks of improvements or buildings from lot lines, and maximum lot coverage.

City Hall is your ally. The high quality of services and people available to you at City Hall are indispensable to your real property decisions. Santa Fe publishes several helpful brochures outlining property procedures and requirements, but the single most valuable document is the one titled "Chapter Three; Zoning and Related Laws." This is available for a modest fee and should be considered part of your investment in your real estate.

This "zoning book" describes all areas, from residential to commercial to industrial. It will indicate the permissible variety of uses in each zoning, under current regulation. But even those of us who use this "zoning book" regularly and think we understand its

contents will often have questions which require clarification.

Feel free to call or visit your City Hall, which is staffed by well-trained professionals. They work with and for you and your concerns. The Code Enforcement department is a good place to begin with most of your questions. Dean Hunt, a licensed engineer, is head of this department and is a near expert on issues relating to the subdivision of property. Jeanne Price is another name to know if you would like to split or subdivide your parcel.

Also within Code Enforcement is the Zoning Division. Any questions you have regarding zoning and allowable uses should be directed to Eddie Romero. He is both knowledgeable and helpful. Under the Zoning

Division you will find the Building Inspectors where Gil Catanach can assist you with requirements of construction.

City Hall is located at the corner of Lincoln and Marcy streets downtown. Code Enforcement and Zoning are to be found in the west wing, first floor. Do take advantage of the expertise and good will of these professionals, part of our city staff, when considering property decisions.

City development policies, which can also influence your property's future value to you, will be discussed in the next chapter.

Your delight in your property, and its future value, is probably of great importance to you. Did you know that a group whom you employ at City Hall, the Planning Department, is also concerned with the aesthetic and happy enjoyment of people and property within Santa Fe? And so, in some ways, this department affects property values.

First, what is the Planning Department? It is a collection of persons professionally trained to coordinate, control and enhance whatever development occurs within our city. Santa Fe's "General Plan" is our city's development policy. The Planning Department is charged with preparing the "General Plan," keeping it current, and advising on any changes or amendments. Our chief City Planner for the past 18 years has been Harry Moul. He studied planning at MIT and taught at Berkeley in the late 1960s.

Property value is not simply equated with size or square footage. It is also determined by views, open space, clean air, landscaping, and other intangibles. Planning Department support of ordinances that enhance these design qualities will add to your enjoyment and to the value of your property.

One new ordinance, fashioned by Linda Tigges of the Planning Department with the assistance of volunteer advisors, is the Escarpment Ordinance. Escarpment means a steep slope leading to a ridgetop. The intent of this ordinance is to prevent the further scarring of our slopes by thoughtless road cutting. It will also prevent two-story homes from looming large on our ridges. The effect will be to enhance our views as we look toward the mountains. There will be less visual interruption in these views than would be the case without this ordinance. And the preservation of our views adds to the value of our lives and property.

Another issue, nurtured by planner Marian Shirin, is our Open Space Plan, approved by the City Council in 1987. This plan is designed to preserve our trails to city land and the national forest. It will also add new trails and open spaces to allow and to support further non-motorized recreation of all sorts. Other locales with open space plans have found their cities more desirable places in which to live. They have also found that properties near or at open spaces tend to increase in value.

Santa Fe's Planning Department is not specifically concerned with an individual's property enhancement. However, their professional care for the city as a whole works to preserve value by any measurement.

Do you have a shoe box full of large bills in U.S. currency? Or a plump bank account? If not, yet you contemplate the purchase of real property in Santa Fe, consider using O.P.M. or Other People's Money.

O.P.M., in this context, translates into what is known as a loan for the purpose of buying real estate. Your lender may be your seller or an institution such as a bank, savings and loan, or a group of investors. If the seller is the lender, the O.P.M. is his equity (savings) in the property which you are not giving back to him quite yet, but over a period of time. The O.P.M. in an institutional loan is the savings of many individuals unknown to you.

In the Santa Fe area, two methods of financing or lending are most common. One is the Real Estate Contract (REC). The other is the mortgage. If the seller finances your purchase of his or her property he may use either of these methods. An institutional lender will only use a mortgage.

What are some of the differences between the Real Estate Contract and the mortgage? And how are these differences relevant to you, the purchaser?

When you use a mortgage as your financing instrument you have received legal title to the property, by virtue of the deed signed to you by the seller. Your mortgage does not then pass title to the lender (mortgagee) or back to the seller if he is the lender, but does create a lien against your property in favor of the lender. This lien is only cleared upon full repayment of your loan. Your promise to pay the loan is evidenced by a promissory note, signed by you, the borrower or mortgagor. Upon repayment of the amount borrowed, be sure to record a "release of mortgage" in the county courthouse. This release, signed by your lender, will then cancel the mortgage (lien) recorded earlier by him. Also, the Promissory note should be marked "PAID" by your lender.

With an REC as your method of financing you agree to receive a deed at a later date. At closing, you receive the right of possession and equitable title. The seller will control legal title should you default on your payments. However, when all the conditions of your REC are fulfilled, not the least of which is to pay your indebtedness in full, you will receive legal title or a General Warranty Deed. Again, record this deed as well as the release of the REC in the county courthouse. Incidentally, the REC is the promise to pay, so a separate promissory note is not used.

Both a mortgage and an REC will contain language about "default" or your non-payment of the amount borrowed. They will describe what is required to "cure" or make up for the default, including the length of your grace period. If you do not "cure" your default under a mortgage, the lender will proceed with foreclosure through the courts. Even after the foreclosure you, the mortgagor, have the right of redemption, customarily for one month. To redeem your property, all indebtedness and court costs must be paid. Most REC's do not provide for a redemption period

once the deed has been returned to the seller after default.

In Santa Fe it is not uncommon for your seller to act as your lender. This financing source has many advantages, at least in the short run. The interest rate charged is generally below institutional rates. And you do not come out of pocket for charges such as loan applications, appraisals, origination fees and "points." The down-side, however, is that a seller is not normally in a position to carry your loan for a long period of time. In a very few years you will need to produce the balance due on your indebtedness. This seems simple upon closing but less so as the due date looms large.

Consideration of types and sources of financing is probably not a pleasurable high point in your purchase of property here. But an informed choice, with knowledge of alternate consequences, can ensure happy sleeping patterns.

Are you about to submit an offer to purchase property? If so, you are probably excited and anxious. If the current market is one of strong demand and little supply you may also feel a sense of urgency lest someone else buy this parcel before you.

However, this is a time to contain your emotions with a measure of caution. Consider carefully which safeguards and disclosures should be contained in your offer to purchase. Your broker and/or attorney are indispensable guides in this process and can help avoid unpleasant surprises at closing.

This and ensuing chapters highlight some subjects which should be entertained in your offer.

A common question is what will be included in the purchase price, in addition to the land and structure? Which appliances or fixtures do you hope or expect to remain with the property? We assume that "fixed and attached" items will stay, but the chandelier may hold special meaning for the seller. The range may be considered a drop-in type rather than "fixed and attached." The expression ALL APPLIANCES may seem straightforward wording in a contract. But sellers have been known to remove a washer, dryer, and freezer any-

way, claiming that they weren't individually mentioned. In short, be as specific as possible in drafting your offer.

Earnest Money, or a deposit to show that your proposal is earnest, is not required in an offer to purchase in this area. However, it is customary and expected by the seller. You may exhibit your earnestness with a gaggle of geese, a coin collection, or U.S. dollars. If you offer dollars, ask where your earnest money will be deposited. In the listing broker's trust account? This is typical, but such accounts are not permitted to yield interest. If your closing date is far in the future, you may want the funds in another account, one which pays interest. Be sure to specify to whom and under what circumstances the interest will be paid to you or the seller.

Most often your *ability* to complete your purchase will be conditional upon the willingness of a lender to make funds available to you. Outline carefully in your offer the amount you need to borrow, along with a term and interest rate acceptable to you. If the lender's proposal does not meet your financing condition or contingency as written in your offer, your earnest money should be returned to you and your offer voided. Of course, it is your option to accept a higher interest rate than the one detailed in your financing contingency.

Your *willingness* to complete your purchase, as distinct from your ability, may depend on other factors intrinsic to the property. These conditions or questions should also be included in your offer to purchase. For example, is the building sound? Is the well water production adequate and potable? Is the slope buildable? In Santa Fe the burden is customarily on the buyer to provide and pay for pertinent inspections and expert opinions. The results of these inspections must be acceptable to you, in your sole discretion. Again, if you declare the results unacceptable, and do so in writing, you should be able to retrieve your earnest money deposit and terminate the offer.

Ensuing chapters will raise questions of easements, zoning, surveys, title insurance and other issues of concern in your offer to purchase.

The last chapter explored financing and inspection contingencies to be considered in your agreement to purchase property. There are other areas of concern with which you should be comfortable. In your offer, retain the right of approval of all legal details pertinent to the property. Any property may be burdened with easements and restrictions. Request a preliminary title insurance policy (the title binder) which will make reference to such things if they have been recorded at the Santa Fe County Courthouse. Ask the title company for a copy of the document which describes these inhibitions on the property so that you can determine their significance. Does a utility easement run under the best building site and so preclude that location for your home construction? Or do the neighbors have the right to cross your land and would this be a bother to you?

Private restrictive covenants or restrictions on the use of the property may eliminate this particular parcel's desirability. Look for building height restrictions, the number and type of pets allowed, a limit on deciduous landscaping or water usage, or extraordinary setbacks from the lot lines. In short, make sure that you can use and enjoy the property in the way you anticipate. Inquire further about general building requirements and zoning restrictions. What do the building codes say about the height of your garden wall? Is the parcel large enough to allow a septic tank if no sewer exists? Can you build a bridge across an arroyo for improved access? Is the slope of the land too steep to be buildable?

Are you planning to add a guest house and would this be a crucial aspect of your purchase? Currently the county's policy concerning guest quarters is a bit fuzzy. You would be wise to inquire directly at the County Courthouse on Grant Street. The City of Santa Fe updated its guest house regulations in September 1988. One key element is that the guest house or "accessory dwelling unit" may not exceed heated gross square footage of 1,000 square feet. Also, it may not be higher than the main house and must be of the same architectural style. And again, check the private covenants for any special guest house restrictions.

The purchaser, through the act of buying property, will be assuming the legal burdens of easement, restrictions and zoning, if any, which run with this property. However, you have the right to approve or disapprove them. If you disapprove any of these burdens or constraints and the seller cannot change them, it is recommended that you search for a different property.

Some legal constraints on property were discussed in the preceding chapter. A carefully drafted offer to purchase should allow for your exploration of and approval or disapproval of such constraints.

Many other elements in your offer are worthy of consideration, whether you use the Board of Realtors' contract form or that of your broker or attorney.

One is that the seller provide evidence that the parcel is not in a flood boundary or zone. While river frontage land is a delight to the eye, especially in the Santa Fe area, you need to know if a building permit will be issued. Also, lenders frown on their equity washing downstream with the occasional flood.

What extra costs of purchase will you be expected to bear? Generally, any cost related to obtaining your financing will be your expenditure, as well as those incurred by recording documents in the County Courthouse which protect your ownership rights. It is customary in Santa Fe for the buyer and seller to split the title company closing fee.

In your offer you can expect proration at closing of such expenses as county property tax, city refuse and sewer assessments, and rent if a tenant is occupying the premises. In Santa Fe County taxes are paid in arrears. The tax bill is due in December and covers the period from the prior January 1st. If your closing occurs on July 1, your seller will pay to you the tax amount incurred from the first of the year, in this case, half of the year's tax bill since he had use of the property for this time. This amount will be "guesstimated" based on the prior year's tax amount.

Does your agreement or offer clarify the "date of closing"? Is it the day on which you sign closing documents or the day you or your lender pay for the property and the title is transferred to you? This can be significant if these days are not the same. If your agreement calls for "possession" on the day of closing, it would be wise to clarify the term "closing."

If a tenant is residing in or using the property, your agreement should call for the seller to give legal and written notice to vacate. Otherwise your "date of possession" may not be enforceable even though you are now the owner. Whether or not the tenant stays on should be your choice and not become a problem through omission.

The next chapter will discuss further your title insurance policy, what can happen if you change your mind, counter offers, and the use of facsimile machines. If the multiplicity of subjects to be covered in your offer seems a bit staggering, remember that your broker and attorney are accustomed to these important details. So whenever possible, use their services.

The seller will be providing you with a Title Insurance policy. In addition to policy protection relating to easements and rights of parties in possession, discussed earlier, you will need two other areas protected by your title policy. Request that your seller provide survey and lien protection. This will mean that your title policy will guarantee against a faulty survey of your property and that no surprise liens or claims for payment will surface after you purchase. A title policy of this quality means that your title insuror will defend a neighbor's claim that part of your land is his or a roofer's claim that he wasn't paid for work done for the seller.

Request, as part of your offer, that the seller provide a disclosure statement as to the known defects of the property. Many Santa Fe brokers are now requiring such a signed statement as part of their listing contracts. This list should include things such as structural or mechanical, plumbing, and heating problems, radon testing, well data, or information on recent repairs. It should also include disclosures relevant to the property but not part of it. For example, is the parcel on or near an anticipated Waste Isolation Pilot Project route? Is the escarpment ordinance in force if the ridge top is included in your land? In short, anything relating to your future use or enjoyment which is known by the seller should be disclosed to you.

An area of confusion and often of disappointment is that of response to your offer by the seller. Until the seller accepts your offer, in writing and without a single change, he or she is free to accept an offer from anyone else. You also, until acceptance, are free to withdraw your offer. If the seller changes the smallest item in your offer, it becomes a counter offer and you are again both free to withdraw or go elsewhere. If and when you both agree to changes in counter offers, be sure to initial or sign and date each change so there is no confusion as to a meeting of the minds. Some attorneys believe that a contract should require both written acceptance and *delivery* to the other party. Do clarify this distinction in your purchase agreement if you do expect delivery.

In New Mexico, verbal agreements or contracts are generally acceptable but not enforceable except in such cases as leases for less than a year. The more written clarification in your offer, the better.

The availability of facsimile (FAX) machines tempts us to respond to contracts of all sorts in a more immediate fashion. But of course a "Faxed" response cannot bear an *original* signature. If you anticipate the use of FAX in your negotiations, indicate in your offer that you will accept facsimile documents as binding until such time as they can be replaced by original signatures, but certainly before closing.

What if, after all your conditions have been proven to your satisfaction, you simply change your mind and choose not to proceed with your contracts? Is your earnest money forfeited to the seller as "liquidated damages?" This is a payment to the seller for his efforts and for keeping his property off the market when it might have sold to another. Or does your offer/contract allow for "specific performance"? In this case the seller could legally require you to purchase the property regardless of your current desires. Do read your offer to purchase carefully and ensure that you are comfortable with this distinction.

This four-chapter check list for buyers is by no means a complete one. Questions and issues are in a constant state of flux. Consult your broker and your attorney for additional ideas and safeguards.

The prior four chapters discussed which elements should be included in your offer to purchase real property here in Santa Fe. These ideas were intended to protect all parties to the transaction. Further, they were designed so that you, the buyer, could be assured as to the quality of the property you are about to own and enjoy. Throughout the book I encouraged you to consult your broker and your attorney for "additional ideas and safeguards." And a consistent theme was to not allow anxiety or a sense of urgency to cloud your deliberations.

Didn't all these recommendations sound reasonable and logical? I thought so, yet while finishing these four chapters I fell in love with a property. Not reasonable or logical . . . just in love. For the first time in nineteen years I was willing to leave my beloved old adobe. This is not only an historic structure (originally a dance hall) so designated by the New Mexico Historic Division but the home in which my sons grew to adulthood.

The new object of my affections is a corny, funky "fifties" house. Its additions are of very marginal quality and there is insufficient wall space for my furniture. Electrical and plumbing are inadequate and the roof

begs to be replaced. But I love it. The grounds are wonderful and bear great promise. The original owner thoughtfully planted and tended exotic trees and shrubs. And the mountain views invite thoughts of magic mornings.

All of this enthusiasm has pushed me over the hill, has led me to violate most of the logical recommendations I so earnestly urged on you. Although an experienced broker in my seventeenth year in business, I suffered giant waves of anxiety and urgency. Would someone else love this property as much as I and buy it first? Where were the sellers and when would they respond to my very earnest offer? Their representative said they were in Austria. Of course, I expected an instant phone call placed to them. This was done, only to discover that they had just left for Russia. "Russia?

Well, phone them," say I. No anxiety here . . . just the calm, measured approach I recommended to you! They were reached in that distant country and promised a response in a week. A WEEK of sleepless nights! My son, Patrick, was thrilled. He now feels I can empathize more fully with our buyers!

But anxiety and urgency weren't the only violations against my strictures to you. Did I consult my attorney or the experienced people in my own office? Of course not. This overwhelming sense of urgency led me to hand-draft the offer while sitting in the office of the sellers' attorney! Fortunately, our purchase agreement form includes enough safeguards that I could not give away the store.

Most brokers are extremely careful in acting for and advising others. But some of us are quite remiss when we act on our own account. Please, valued readers, do as I say, not as I do.

What is a "closing" in the Santa Fe area? Who attends and why? What happens and where does it happen?

In Santa Fe a closing means that time at which a buyer and seller of real property sit down to review and sign final documents necessary to the transaction.

Both parties will peruse and sign their respective "closing statements" which are lists of debits and credits, monies paid out or received in the process of the purchase and sale.

The seller will sign a deed, granting the property to the buyer. The buyer will sign a check for the purchase amount or provide a cashier's check. More likely the buyer will be borrowing funds to purchase the property and so will sign a ream of loan documents, each more abstruse than the last.

Who pulls together all these documents, preparing some and reviewing all for accuracy? The Title Insurance Company "closing officer" who in most cases is professional and knowledgeable. Some are attorneys as well, with a specialty in real property issues. The closing officer will lead you through the transaction and ensure that the appropriate documents are recorded afterward in our county courthouse.

Your attorney is not required to be present at closing, as is the case in some northeastern states. However, his or her presence is advisable if there is the slightest complexity in your transaction.

If you enlist the aid of a broker in your sale or purchase, that broker will also be with you, for further analysis and review of the documents. Incidentally, you need not be present for your closing to occur. If all the documents have been signed and notarized in advance, and received by the closing officer, he can finalize and record the transaction without you.

Most buyers assume that upon signing all the closing documents they have become the new owner of the property. But if your purchase requires funds from a bank, savings and loan or underwriter, that lender will require inspection of all the documents signed at closing before releasing the funds to the seller. So even

though the seller has signed the deed to you at closing, that deed is held in escrow or trust until the borrowed funds are available to the seller. With this scenario you may close on a Friday but not receive the title until the following Tuesday or Wednesday. In short, closing and ownership may not be simultaneous.

In the early 1970s, closing in Santa Fe occurred anywhere, in a restaurant or a broker's office. The "closing statement" may have been casually typed on the broker's letterhead. In one incident in which I was the buyer the broker embellished the event with cheese, bread and wine! Today our slightly more formal closings take place in the title company's office. But while more structured and formal (and careful) you can still expect the event to be casual and comfortable. Rather than anticipating a legal trauma think of your closing as the beginning of a new chapter.

What might a buyer from Boston or one from Beverly Hills have in common upon the purchase of real property in the Santa Fe area? Each may soon learn the strength of the words "acequia," or irrigation ditch, and of a community acequia association.

If you find yourself the purchaser of property which includes ditch or "acequia" rights, you are thrice blessed. You can experience the American Indian and European technology of irrigation, the latter refined to a great extent during the Moors' occupation of Spain. You are entering an historical and communal neighborhood society. And, given a wet year, you will have some use of surface water for your vegetable and fruit endeavors.

In New Mexico the state owns the water, more valuable than whiskey. You may, however, by means of your ditch rights have the right to some *use* of water. This water must be applied or used in a "beneficial way" and can be lost by lack of use.

Acequias or ditch associations in New Mexico are seen as political subdivisions of the state. They have the power to assess and borrow for improvements and maintenance; they may sue or be sued. Anyone interfer-

ing with an acequia or using water without permission of the mayordomo or ditch boss faces fines and, statutorily, the possibility of jail! As Ignacio Moya, the late mayordomo of Santa Fe's Acequia Madre once said, "The Acequia Madre has more power than the president of the United States." An exaggeration perhaps, but not in its historical context.

Your deed will make reference to your ditch rights, if any, and should describe the amount of your land entitled to the water. However, your irrigation possibilities could be diminished depending on the amount of surface water available from one year to the next.

Acequias are under the general control of commissioners (comisionados) and a mayordomo, elected by you and other members of your acequia association. Think of the mayordomo as the chief executive officer and make friends with him. He is the one who decides the timing of water distribution. If you are tardy in paying your dues or in providing "trabajo," or work on the ditches, you may find the time for the diversion of water onto your land to be 2 to 4 a.m.!!

One right of the acequia which might puzzle the new resident in Santa Fe is the right of easement. The acequia association has both an easement for the ditch carrying the water and for the amount of land historically used on each bank for maintenance. The mayordomo is guaranteed access to both. These easements are inviolate, even if your property has no rights from a ditch bordering or crossing your land. Recently, a new homeowner in the upper Canyon Road area began a bedroom enlargement which would have infringed on the acequia easement. He re-drew his plans!

To fully enjoy your acequia, its rights and responsibilities you may need to develop an unaccustomed communal attitude. Your acequia is a privilege, not a violation of property rights. And with it "runs" the opportunity to meet neighbors and "parciantes," or water users, some of whom have been irrigating from this ditch for fifty years.

One point of view is that land or property cannot be 'owned' — at least not in the sense that we own personal or ephemeral property or things. This land, all land was here before us and, with luck and our attention, will survive us. Perhaps our idea or ownership should be reduced to a sense of caretaking or nurturing and enhancing.

If you plan to purchase the right to caretake the land here, these chapters may have offered some insights to peculiarities of the Santa Fe area.

For further and more detailed information, contact the appropriate department in the City or County of Santa Fe:

CITY:
City Zoning	984-6658
Code Enforcement	984-6646
Planning Department	984-6605

COUNTY:
County Land Use	984-5025

STATE OF NEW MEXICO:
State Engineer	827-6120